ANIMALS IN ORDER

Erin Pembrey Swan

Land Predators of North America

Franklin Watts - A Division of Grolier Publishing

New York • London • Hong Kong • Sydney • Danbury, Connecticut

For Henry, because he is a land predator

Photographs ©: ENP Images: 15 (Gerry Ellis), 41 right (Steve Gettle), 37 (Terry Whittaker), 5 top left, 6, 35 (Konrad Wothe); Lynn M. Stone: cover, 5 bottom left, 13, 19, 21, 25, 38, 39; Photo Researchers: 43 (E.R. Degginger), 5 bottom right (Maslowski), 42 center (Jim Zipp); Tony Stone Images: 27, 32, 33 (Daniel J. Cox), 1 (Peter Pearson), 30, 31 (Tom Ulrich); Visuals Unlimited: 29 (S. Maslowski), 7 (Joe McDonald); Wildlife Collection: 40, 41 left (Bob Bennett), 17, 23, 42, (Michael Francis), 5 top right (D. Robert Pranz).

Illustrations by Jose Gonzales and Steve Savage

Visit Franklin Watts on the Internet at:
http://publishing.grolier.com

Library of Congress Cataloging-in-Publication Data

Swan, Erin Pembrey
Land predators of North America / Erin Pembrey Swan.
    p. cm. — (Animals in order)
    Includes bibliographical references and index.
    Summary: Introduces and identifies fourteen North American land predators, including bears, skunks, and weasels, and offers recommendations for tracking them.
    ISBN 0-531-11451-1 (lib. bdg.)   0-531-15945-0 (pbk)
    1. Predatory animals—Juvenile literature. 2. Animal tracks—Juvenile literature.
[1. Predatory animals. 2. Animal tracks. 3. Animals—Habitats and behavior.]   I. Title.
II. Series.
QL758.S79   1999
599.15'3—dc21
                                                                                        98-2705
                                                                                        CIP
                                                                                        AC

© 1999 Franklin Watts
Printed in the United States of America.
    3 4 5 6 7 8 9 10 R 08 07 06 05 04

GROLIER
PUBLISHING

Contents

What Is a
Land Predator?

Have you ever watched a cat catch a mouse? Belly to the ground, it creeps toward its unsuspecting *prey*—slowly, slowly, closer and closer. A wriggle of its rear end, a tensing of its muscles, and then POUNCE! It grabs the mouse with its long, sharp claws.

A house cat is one kind of land *predator*. Although most house cats are fed by humans and don't have to hunt for food, many do anyway. The group, or *order*, of animals called "land predators" have two very important things in common. They all live on land, and they all kill and eat other animals to survive.

Three of the four animals on the next page are land predators. Can you tell which one is not?

Bear

Beaver

Skunk

Weasel

Traits of a Land Predator

Did you pick the beaver? You were right! How could you tell it is not a land predator?

Land predators hunt other animals for food, so they need to have built-in "weapons." Most have sharp teeth and claws. A beaver is a rodent, not a land predator. Its long, square front teeth are perfect for gnawing, but they are not much good for attacking prey.

Bears, skunks, weasels, and other land predators use their teeth to kill prey and tear it apart. Their *canine teeth* are long, large, and pointed. These fanglike teeth help the predator keep a tight grip on its victim until the helpless animal dies. The predator then uses these sharp teeth to carry the prey to a safe eating place. Most land predators have four *carnassial teeth*—two on the bottom and two on the top—made especially for tearing meat from their victims' bodies. They are kind of like having a built-in knife and fork.

Many land predators also have very sharp claws. The claws of most cats are *retractile*.

This means they can be pulled into the paw to make it soft and gentle or pushed out to transform the paw into a dangerous weapon. Although some other land predators have sharp claws, they are not retractile and are not generally used during hunting.

All land predators have an excellent sense of smell, sharp eyesight, and sensitive hearing. They are usually strong and very fast. All these traits help them hunt for food. Most land predators hunt alone or in pairs, but some, like wolves and lions, hunt in groups.

Land predators give birth to several babies at one time. These groups of tiny, blind young are called litters. The young quickly grow into a furry bunch of eager hunters.

The Order of Living Things

A tiger has more in common with a house cat than with a daisy. A true bug is more like a butterfly than a jellyfish. Scientists arrange living things into groups based on how they look and how they act. A tiger and a house cat belong to the same group, but a daisy belongs to a different group.

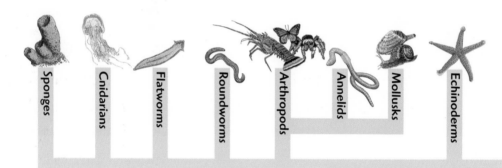

Sponges Cnidarians Flatworms Roundworms Arthropods Annelids Mollusks Echinoderms

Animals

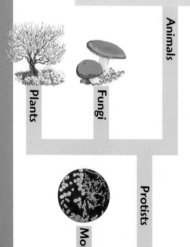

Plants Fungi

Protists

Monerans

All living things can be placed in one of five groups called *kingdoms*: the plant kingdom, the animal kingdom, the fungus kingdom, the moneran kingdom, or the protist kingdom. You can probably name many of the creatures in the plant and animal kingdoms. The fungus kingdom includes mushrooms, yeasts, and molds. The moneran and protist kingdoms contain thousands of living things that are too small to see without a microscope.

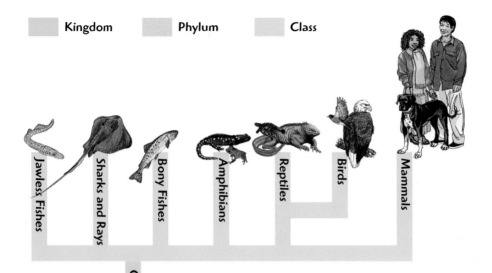

Kingdom   Phylum   Class

Jawless Fishes

Sharks and Rays

Bony Fishes

Amphibians

Reptiles

Birds

Mammals

Chordates

Because there are millions and millions of living things on Earth, some of the members of one kingdom may not seem all that similar. The animal kingdom includes creatures as different as tarantulas and trout, jellyfish and jaguars, salamanders and sparrows, elephants and earthworms.

To show that an elephant is more like a jaguar than an earthworm, scientists further separate the creatures in each kingdom into more specific groups. The animal kingdom can be divided into nine *phyla*. Humans belong to the chordate phylum. Almost all chordates have a backbone.

Each phylum can be subdivided into many *classes*. Humans, mice, and elephants all belong to the mammal class. Each class can be further divided into orders; orders into *families*, families into *genera*, and genera into *species*. All the members of a species are very similar.

How Land Predators Fit In

You can probably guess that the land predators belong to the animal kingdom. They have much more in common with bees and bats than with maple trees and morning glories.

Land predators belong to the chordate phylum. Almost all chordates have a backbone and a skeleton. Can you think of other chordates? Examples include elephants, mice, snakes, birds, fish, and whales.

The chordate phylum can be divided into a number of classes. All mammals belong to the same class. Elephants, humans, dogs, and cats are all mammals.

There are seventeen different orders of mammals. The land predators make up one of these orders. The scientific name for this order is "carnivora," which means "flesh eaters." As you learned earlier, all land predators have features that help them capture, kill, and eat other animals.

The land predators can be divided into a number of different families and genera, and many different species. Land predators live in all kinds of *habitats* and on every continent except Antarctica. In this book, you will learn more about some of the land predators that live in North America.

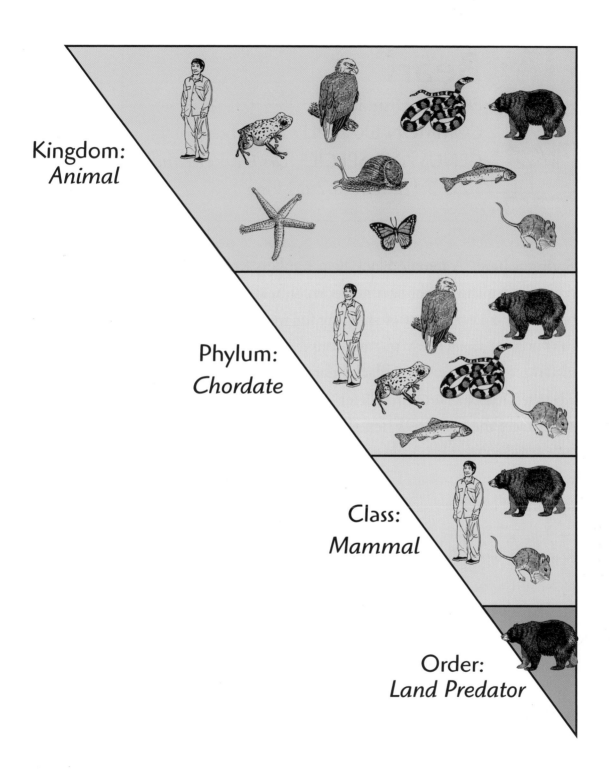

Kingdom:
Animal

Phylum:
Chordate

Class:
Mammal

Order:
Land Predator

Bears

FAMILY: Ursidae
COMMON EXAMPLE: Black bear
GENUS AND SPECIES: *Ursus americanus*
SIZE: 5 1/2 feet (1.7 m) long

Spring is here! A female black bear lumbers from her winter den to greet the sunshine, her two newborn cubs stumbling along behind her. After a long winter of sleeping for weeks at a time, the mother bear is more than ready to run around.

To prepare for winter, black bears spend most of the fall eating. This helps them build up a layer of fat that nourishes them as they sleep away the winter. When the weather starts to get really cold, bears find a cozy den and settle down to snooze. Every once in a while, they wake up and spend a few hours poking about in the snow for food. Then they return to their warm den for another long nap.

Young bears are born in late winter. Most of the time, a mother bear gives birth to two cubs. Newborn cubs are tiny—small enough to fit in the palm of your hand. But they grow quickly, gaining about 40 pounds (18 kg) during their first summer. After about a year and a half with their mother, the young bears are ready for life on their own.

Bears catch and eat small animals and often feed on animals that are already dead. They also feed on roots, bulbs, grass, wild berries, acorns, fruit, and, of course, honey.

Martens

FAMILY: Mustelidae
EXAMPLE: American marten
GENUS AND SPECIES: *Martes americana*
SIZE: 22 inches (56 cm)

A hungry marten is chasing a red squirrel. The squirrel is fast, but the marten is faster. With one quick pounce and a snap of its teeth, the marten turns the squirrel into a tasty lunch.

Red squirrels are its favorite food, but a marten eats many other things too. It hunts mice, rabbits, birds, and insects. It may also eat berries, nuts, and birds' eggs if it is really hungry. With its speed and excellent climbing skills, a marten usually has no trouble catching prey. If it cannot eat its prey in one sitting, it hides the carcass until it is hungry again.

The American marten lives in the northern spruce and balsam forests of North America. It spends most of its time in the trees—hunting, sleeping, and raising its young. It sleeps during the day in a leafy nest built inside a log or a hollow tree. At night, the marten comes out to hunt. Martens hunt alone, and each one marks its hunting area with a strong scent that comes from glands under its tail. This scent tells other martens to KEEP AWAY!

Skunks

FAMILY: Mustelidae
COMMON EXAMPLE: Common skunk
GENUS AND SPECIES: *Mephitis mephitis*
SIZE: 25 inches (63.5 cm)

Watch out! Alarmed by an overeager dog, a skunk stamps its front feet and waves its bushy tail. Is that dog still coming? The skunk turns, lifts its tail, and sprays a stinky, oily mist all over the horrified dog. Tail between its legs, the dog runs home.

If a skunk is attacked or even startled, it sprays everything in its path. The bad-smelling yellow spray can hit objects up to 10 feet (3 m) away. Although the victim's eyes may burn for a while, the liquid does not cause any permanent damage. But the spray's horrible, strong smell can last for several days.

Striped skunks will eat almost anything—earthworms, mice, or even a tasty bit of meat from your garbage can.

Young skunks are born in the spring. The newborns have no hair, but the light and dark markings on their skin show where their furry stripes will be. While some skunks leave their mother when they are about 4 months old, others stay with her through the winter.

Wolverines

FAMILY: Mustelidae
COMMON NAME: Wolverine
GENUS AND SPECIES: *Gulo gulo*
SIZE: 44 inches (112 cm)

A wolverine is digging into a rabbit *burrow*. Soon all the rabbits inside that burrow will be lunch for the hungry wolverine. When it is too full to eat any more, the wolverine will hide what's left over for another meal.

Wolverines live in the northern regions of Europe, Asia, and North America. Luckily, they have a long, dark coat to keep them warm. These animals are known for their big appetites.

Whether they're digging rabbits out of a burrow or attacking a snowbound caribou, wolverines are strong and clever enough to make up for their small size and short legs. In the summer, they eat anything they can find—berries, plants, mice, rabbits, and birds. During the long winters, they live off weak or dead animals. Moving quickly across deep snow on their wide, furry paws, they pounce on deer, elk, or caribou stuck in snowdrifts. When wolverines get very hungry, they will even eat animals caught in traps set by humans.

Wolves

FAMILY: Canidae
EXAMPLE: Gray wolf
GENUS AND SPECIES: *Canis lupus*
SIZE: 68 inches (172.5 cm)

A long, lonely howl splits the silence of a winter night. A wolf stands on a hill, calling for his lost friends. The howl says, "I'm over here. Come find me!" Wolves talk to each other by howling. The howls may mean "I'm lost," or "Go away, stranger!" Or they may be a call for all friendly wolves to get together after a hunt.

Gray wolves live in groups called packs. The strongest male in the pack is called the *alpha male*. As the leader, he controls all the other wolves. His mate—the alpha female—controls the females. The whole pack hunts together, using teamwork to attack caribou, elk, and other large animals. When they can't find large prey, wolves will fill up on smaller animals, such as mice.

These wolves can be found in the northern forests of North America, but you will probably never see one in the wild. They are very rare. In the past, many were killed by farmers because they killed their sheep or chickens. Many others died because the forests where they lived were destroyed to make room for industry or housing developments. Today, wolves are protected by laws. They are free to roam the hills and forests once more, howling their messages at the sky.

Bobcats

FAMILY: Felidae
COMMON NAME: Bobcat
GENUS AND SPECIES: *Lynx rufus*
SIZE: 33 inches (83.5 cm)

It is midnight. Two bobcat kittens follow their mother into the dark forest, creeping after her through the underbrush. The spring air is alive with the sounds of animals moving all around. Although the kittens are only 3 months old, they have grown quickly and are now big enough to hunt for themselves. This is their first time, and they are ready!

The young bobcats will hunt with their mother all summer. As the weather grows colder, they will begin to hunt on their own. Soon they will leave their mother to find their own mates, make their own dens, and have their own babies.

Full-grown bobcats are expert hunters. They eat anything from a snowshoe hare to a squirrel to a bluejay. The largest northern bobcats can bring down a running deer.

Bobcats are the most common wildcats in North America. They live in forests, on hills, and in swamps. They are sometimes seen in open farmland. Because they can survive on a diet of small animals and can live almost anywhere, bobcats have not been pushed out by people. Some even live happily near large cities!

Cougars

FAMILY: Felidae

COMMON NAME: Cougar or mountain lion

GENUS AND SPECIES: *Felis concolor*

SIZE: 8 feet (2.5 m) (female smaller)

A cougar crouches silently and peers into the night. It has spotted a deer drinking at a nearby stream. Quietly, quietly, the cougar creeps toward the deer. Suddenly, the cougar leaps forward, throwing all its weight against the deer and knocking its victim to the ground. Then the cougar sinks its teeth into the deer's neck, and the fight is over. The cougar will eat well tonight.

The cougar is a secretive, solitary cat. Its range extends from southern Canada to the tip of South America. It can live in deserts, mountains, plains, and woodlands. Cougars used to live all over North America, but they were hunted so heavily in the eastern United States that they are now rare in that region. There are still plenty of cougars in the western United States, however.

Cougars prefer deer, but they also eat many other animals. These mighty hunters can catch almost any animal—raccoons, skunks, armadillos, birds, even alligators. A male cougar may roam as far as 25 miles (40 km) in a single night. Cougars usually hunt on the ground, zigzagging through dense thickets and hiding in the shadows.

Cougars also eat sheep, pigs, and cows. That's why so many angry farmers have hunted them over the years.

Raccoons

FAMILY: Procyonidae
COMMON EXAMPLE: North American raccoon
GENUS AND SPECIES: *Procyon lotor*
SIZE: 32 inches (81 cm)

What was that crash? Two hungry raccoons have just tipped over a garbage can. Dinner is served! Whether it's your garbage or a crayfish fresh from a stream, raccoons can make a meal out of it. After sunset, they pop out of their dens to begin their foraging. They look in creeks for frogs and crayfish. They raid birds' nests for eggs. They catch mice, worms, and insects. The bravest raccoons wander into towns to check out garbage cans and dumpsters. Others creep into farmyards in search of chickens or apples.

Raccoons can live almost anywhere. They can make their dens in hollow trees, rock crevices, or even between hay bales in a barn. Some raccoons live in towns and cities, too. Their homes can be in chimneys, attics, old buildings, or large drainpipes. No matter where they are, raccoons make themselves right at home.

Raccoons are excellent climbers. If young raccoons are attacked, their mother sends them scurrying up a tree. Then the mother runs in another direction, leading the enemy away from her babies. Safe in the tree, the baby raccoons wait for their mother to return.

Weasels

FAMILY: Mustelidae
EXAMPLE: Long-tailed weasel
GENUS AND SPECIES: *Mustela frenata*
SIZE: 16 inches (40.5 cm)

A hawk swoops down to attack a long-tailed weasel as it runs across the snow. The weasel's brown fur turned snowy white at the beginning of winter, but the sharp-eyed hawk has spotted the black tip of the weasel's tail. The hawk dives at the black fur, but misses the weasel's *camouflaged* body. The weasel gets away!

Weasels are active all day and all night. They take short naps whenever they feel tired, and they hunt whenever they are hungry. Long-tailed weasels hunt mice, rabbits, chipmunks, and squirrels. If no one is looking, they will creep into chicken coops and kill more chickens than they can eat. Like other land predators, a weasel marks its hunting grounds with a liquid released from scent glands under its tail.

Weasels live in meadows or open woods. They are very fast and very sneaky. These land predators often dig shallow dens under tree roots. Their long, slim bodies can squirm into small places, so sometimes they find shelter in cracks between rocks.

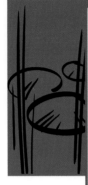

Minks

FAMILY: *Mustelidae*
COMMON NAME: Mink
GENUS AND SPECIES: *Mustela vison*
SIZE: 21 inches (53.5 cm)

What a nice night for a swim! A mink slips into a stream and swims easily to the opposite shore. It climbs out, shakes its fur dry, and crawls into its cozy burrow under the roots of a tree. Its fur-lined bed is the perfect place to spend the long, bright day.

Minks live throughout North America, from Florida to the Arctic Circle. Some live near forest streams; others live in marshes or tidal flats. Minks live close to water because that's where they find their food. Muskrats are their favorite meal, but they also hunt frogs, crayfish, birds, snakes, fish, and mice. If minks catch more than they can eat, they hide it until they are hungry again.

Minks have many enemies, including owls, bobcats, and foxes. When a mink feels

30

threatened, it fluffs up its fur to make itself look bigger, hisses fierce-ly, and rushes at its enemy. That strategy works against some preda-tors, but it is useless against humans who trap minks for their beautiful fur. Some people raise minks on special farms and sell their fur to make expensive coats.

Otters

FAMILY: Mustelidae
COMMON EXAMPLE: River otter
GENUS AND SPECIES: *Lutra canadensis*
SIZE: 40 inches (102 cm)

An otter slides down a muddy riverbank and makes a mighty splash in the water below. The otter climbs out and immediately runs back up the bank to slide down again. What a fun game! Soon the otter feels hungry and begins to search the river for food.

River otters eat many different types of food. They dive for crayfish and frogs, catch insects, and nibble on plants. They pluck small fish from the water and swallow them whole. If they catch a larger fish, they drag it on shore and eat it more slowly.

Otters spend most of their time in the water. To swim, they move their bodies up and down, paddling away with their webbed back feet. These animals love to play. They swim on their backs, turn somersaults, and dive for pebbles. They even play underwater tag, chasing each other round and round.

32

Every female otter teaches her babies to swim. At first, she carries each one into the water on her back. When the young otter seems comfortable in the water, its mother dives down, forcing the baby to swim for itself. In a few moments, the mother returns to the surface and lets the young otter rest on her back for a while. Then the mother dives again. She does this until the baby can swim on its own.

Badgers

FAMILY: Mustelidae
EXAMPLE: American badger
GENUS AND SPECIES: *Taxidea taxus*
SIZE: 34 inches (86.5 cm)

A badger waddles through the snow, sniffing the ground with its pointed nose. When it comes across a ground squirrel's burrow, the badger scratches at the hole with his strong claws. Then it digs quickly until it finds the squirrel. Lunch is served!

American badgers live in open prairies and flat farmland with few trees. From sunset to sunrise, they search for food. They like ground squirrels best, and prairie dogs, too. They also eat insects, earthworms, snakes, frogs, roots, and fruit. Because they have small, bearlike bodies and short legs, badgers can catch only small animals that live on the ground.

A badger uses its strong legs and claws to dig underground tunnels. At the end of its tunnel, it digs out a large room and lines the walls with clean, dry grass. After a night of hunting, the badger crawls into its burrow and sleeps through the long, hot day. In the north, badgers sleep away the winter in these cozy burrows.

In the past, people used badger fur to make shaving brushes and clothing. Today, badgers are protected by laws.

Foxes

FAMILY: Canidae
COMMON EXAMPLE: North American red fox
GENUS AND SPECIES: *Vulpes fulva*
SIZE: 39 inches (99 cm)

In early April, in a snug den dug in the side of a grassy hill, five newborn fox pups open their eyes for the first time. Born blind a week before, these young foxes are more than ready to get a good look at the world. After another 3 weeks, their brown or gray fur begins to turn red. Soon they'll look just like their parents.

At first, the mother stays with the pups because they need her milk. The father brings the mother all the food she needs. After a couple of weeks, both parents go hunting. Like many other predators, foxes eat as much as they can and give their pups pre-chewed food.

The pups grow quickly. After 5 weeks, they are ready to leave the den. Playful and curious, they learn how to hunt mice, catch birds, eat frogs, and find the tastiest blackberries. By late fall, the young foxes are fully grown and ready to start their own families.

Although most foxes hunt at night, you may see one during the day as it trots through the grass looking for mice or berries. Red foxes are good climbers and often use their claws to climb tree trunks. They are also excellent swimmers and can cross a stream quickly to chase a rabbit or get away from an unfriendly dog.

Coyotes

FAMILY: Canidae
COMMON NAME: Coyote
GENUS AND SPECIES: *Canis latrans*
SIZE: 48 inches (122 cm)

A series of sharp yips splits the cool desert evening. A coyote stands alone, calling out to its friends. The yips turn into a howl, and—one by one—the coyote's friends join in. Soon there is a chorus of howls, rising and falling and rising again. Each evening, these coyotes begin the night by singing together. Just before dawn, they sing together again. It's their way of letting each other know where they are.

Coyotes come out at night, ready to hunt and play under the starry sky. They live together in family groups of parents and children. They play together, but usually hunt alone.

Coyotes will eat almost anything. They prefer mice, ground squirrels, gophers, and woodchucks. But if these animals are in short supply, they will feed on berries, snakes, or insects. In the winter, coyotes watch the sky for circling vultures. They know that where there are vultures, there is a tasty meal to be found.

In Native American stories, the coyote is often called the "trickster." Coyotes are very clever animals. They can live almost anywhere. Because their natural habitat is shrinking, coyotes have moved into wooded areas close to large populations of people.

Looking for Signs of Land Predators

Bear tracks

Can you imagine a fox trotting through the moonlit grass? Or a bear sniffing the air as it moves among the trees? Would you like to see one of these animals for yourself?

The best time to see an animal that hunts at night is in the very early morning, when it may be having one last drink at a stream, or in the evening, when it is just heading out to hunt. But even then, you may never see one. Most land predators are shy creatures that stay away from humans.

This doesn't mean that you can't find out whether these animals are in the area. If you go for a walk in a forest or a field, be sure to take a journal with you. Write down and draw pictures of what you see. Be on the lookout for "signs" of land predators. For example, you can search for their tracks, or footprints. You are most likely to

40

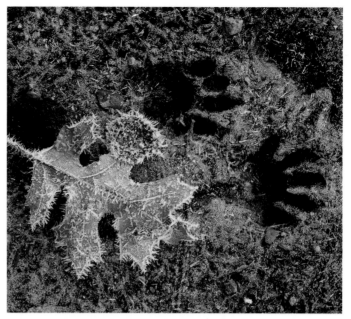

Raccoon tracks

Wolf tracks

see them in fresh snow or in the soft mud near a stream.

You might also see signs of bears on tree trunks. Bears mark their territory by clawing the bark off trees and slashing the trunks with their teeth. They leave long gashes in the tree and a pile of bark strips on the ground. Bears also tear logs apart to find ants. Look for splintered logs with long pieces of wood scattered around them.

You can also look for animal droppings, or *scat*. If it is fresh, the animal was probably there the night before. If it is old and dry, the predator was probably there a few days ago.

Bear scat

Coyote scat

Wolf scat

Bear scat is large. It is usually shaped like thick cylinders, but may be thinner and curvier if the animal has been eating a lot of fruit. Coyote scat is twisted into a point at the ends and may contain the hair of animals the coyote has eaten. Wolf scat is about the same size as coyote scat and also often contains hair. However, wolf scat is more cylindrical and not usually twisted at the ends.

Land predators often leave behind the parts of their prey that they can't eat. If you find clumps of rabbit fur or the bones of a muskrat, a predator was probably there the night before, feasting happily.

Another good way to find land predators is to listen. At night, you might hear a chorus of coyotes or wolves. You can learn a lot by listening carefully to the sounds of the forest and the open prairie.

Words to Know

alpha male—the strongest male in a group of dogs, such as wolves. The alpha male acts as the group's leader.

burrow—a shelter dug in the ground.

camouflage—to hide by blending in with the surrounding environment. For example, a long-tailed weasel's winter fur allows it to blend in with the snow on the ground.

canine teeth—pointed teeth that land predators use to catch and hold their prey.

carnassial teeth—teeth behind the canines that carnivores use to tear flesh from their prey.

class—a group of creatures within a phylum that share certain characteristics.

family—a group of creatures within an order that share certain characteristics.

genus (plural **genera**)—a group of creatures within a family that share certain characteristics.

habitat—the place where an organism is best suited to live.

kingdom—one of the five divisions into which all living things are placed: the animal kingdom, the plant kingdom, the fungus kingdom, the moneran kingdom, and the protist kingdom.

order—a group of creatures within a class that share certain characteristics.

phylum (plural **phyla**)—a group of creatures within a kingdom that share certain characteristics.

predator—an animal that catches and feeds on other animals.

prey—an animal hunted for food by another animal (a predator).

retractile—capable of being drawn back (into the paw).

scat—the solid waste or droppings of an animal.

species—a group of creatures within a genus that share certain characteristics. Members of the same species can mate and produce young.

Learning More

Books

Fair, Jeff. *Raccoons for Kids*. Flagstaff, AZ: Northland Publishing, 1994.

Kudlinski, Kathleen V. *Animal Tracks and Traces*. Danbury, CT: Franklin Watts, 1991.

Parker, Steve. *Amazing Mammals*. New York: Alfred A. Knopf, 1989.

Perry, Phyllis J. *The Snow Cats*. Danbury, CT: Franklin Watts, 1997.

Stirling, Ian. *Bears*. San Francisco: Sierra Club Books, 1995.

Turbak, Gary. *Twilight Hunters: Wolves, Coyotes, and Foxes*. Flagstaff, AZ: Northland Publishing, 1987.

Videos

All American Bear. NOVA Video Library.

Predators of the Wild. Warner Home Video.

Web Sites

The Great Predators Page was developed by the Biology Department of Indiana University of Pennsylvania. It has information on wolves, bears, and cougars. It can be reached at **http://www.envirolink.org/orgs/foa/predator.htm**.

If you're interested in weasels, this site is for you. Find out what they look like, where they live, and how they spend their days. The address is **http://resd.winnipeg.mb.ca/schools/maple.leaf/metclafe.forsyth/weasel347**.

Index

About the Author

Erin Pembrey Swan studied animal behavior, literature, and early childhood education at Hampshire College in Massachusetts. She also studied literature and history at the University College Galway in Ireland. Her poetry has been published in *The Poet's Gallery: The Subterraneans* and *The Poet's Gallery: Voices of Selene* in Woodstock, New York, and in *The Cuirt Journal* in Galway, Ireland. Ms. Swan is also the author of *Primates: From Howler Monkeys to Humans*, another book in the Animals in Order series. Although she lives in New Paltz, New York, Ms. Swan spends a great deal of time traveling to different parts of the world.